CAMELS

Please visit our web site at: www.garethstevens.com
For a free color catalog describing Gareth Stevens Publishing's
list of high-quality books and multimedia programs, call
1-800-542-2595 (USA) or 1-800-387-3178 (Canada).
Gareth Stevens Publishing's fax: (414) 332-3567.

All about camels.
     Camels.
          p. cm. — (All about wild animals)
     Previously published in Great Britain as: All about camels. 2003.
     ISBN 0-8368-4181-6 (lib. bdg.)
     1. Camels —Juvenile literature. I. Title. II. Series.
     QL737.U54A58   2004
     599.63'62—dc22   2004040813

This edition first published in 2005 by
Gareth Stevens Publishing
A World Almanac Education Group Company
330 West Olive Street, Suite 100
Milwaukee, Wisconsin 53212 USA

This U.S. edition copyright © 2005 by Gareth Stevens, Inc. Original edition
copyright © 2003 by DeAgostini UK Limited. First published in 2003 as
My Animal Kingdom: All About Camels by DeAgostini UK Ltd., Griffin House,
161 Hammersmith Road, London W6 8SD, England. Additional end matter
copyright © 2005 by Gareth Stevens, Inc.

Editorial and design: Tucker Slingsby Ltd., London
Gareth Stevens series editor: Catherine Gardner
Gareth Stevens art direction: Tammy West

Picture Credits
NHPA — William Paton: 12—13; Daniel Heuclin: 13; Yves Lanceau: 18, 21;
     Anthony Bannister: 19; Lady Philippa Scott: 24—25; Kevin Schafer: 27 top.
Oxford Scientific Films — Rick Price/SAL: Front cover, title page, 14, 20;
     Eyal Bartov: 6—7; Colin Monteath: 7, 15; Steve Littlewood: 8; John
     Downer: 9; Lee Lyon/SAL: 11; David Curl: 16; Jim Tuten/AA: 17;
     Michael Dick/AA: 19; Mike Brown: 21, 23, 29 bottom; Daniel Cox: 22,
     23 top; Berndt Fischer: 26; David Cayless: 27 bottom; Mike Powles: 28.

Printed in the United States of America

1 2 3 4 5 6 7 8 9 08 07 06 05 04

CAMELS

Gareth Stevens Publishing
A WORLD ALMANAC EDUCATION GROUP COMPANY

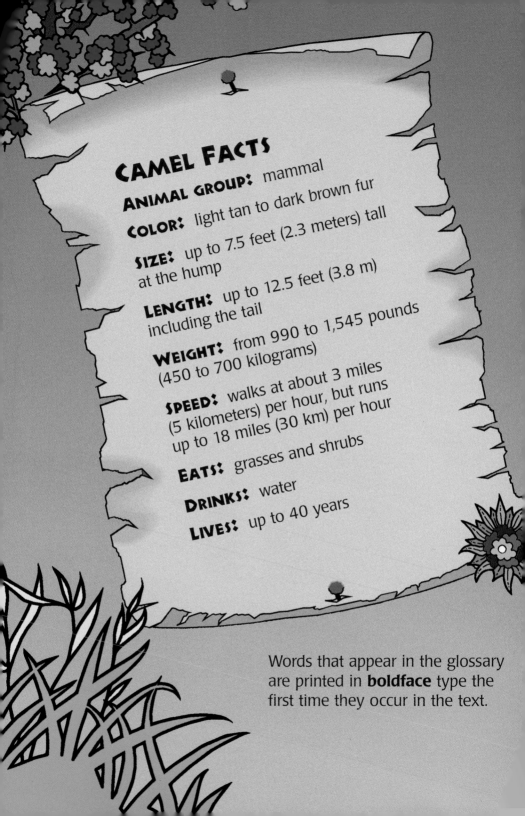

CAMEL FACTS

ANIMAL GROUP: mammal

COLOR: light tan to dark brown fur

SIZE: up to 7.5 feet (2.3 meters) tall at the hump

LENGTH: up to 12.5 feet (3.8 m) including the tail

WEIGHT: from 990 to 1,545 pounds (450 to 700 kilograms)

SPEED: walks at about 3 miles (5 kilometers) per hour, but runs up to 18 miles (30 km) per hour

EATS: grasses and shrubs

DRINKS: water

LIVES: up to 40 years

Words that appear in the glossary are printed in **boldface** type the first time they occur in the text.

Contents

A Closer Look

Camels are well **adapted** to life in a desert. One kind of camel, called a Bactrian camel, has a thick, furry coat that protects it from icy wind in winter and the burning Sun in summer. A Bactrian camel has two humps filled with fat, which it can use for energy when food is **scarce**. It can go for days without eating food or drinking water, and it can walk across deserts on its long, sturdy legs.

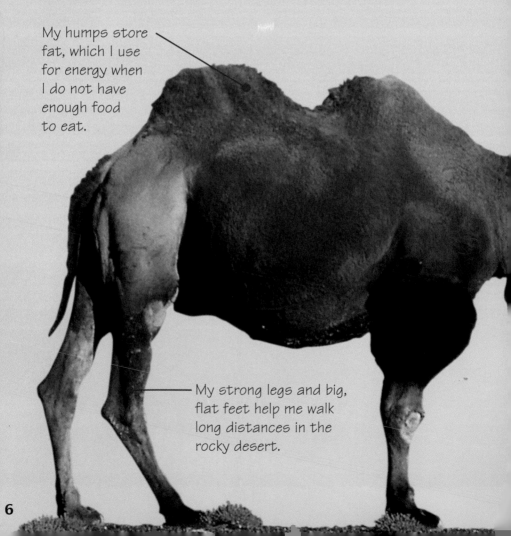

My humps store fat, which I use for energy when I do not have enough food to eat.

My strong legs and big, flat feet help me walk long distances in the rocky desert.

I have a long, curved neck, which helps me stretch for the best plants to eat.

My thick, furry coat keeps me warm at night, but it also can keep me cool on a hot day.

• As a camel walks, it moves both legs on one side of its body and then both legs on the other side. Its walk has the rolling motion of a boat at sea. No wonder camels are called ships of the desert!

• Pads of thick skin cover a camel's knees and protect them when the camel kneels on the ground.

• A camel has large feet with thick, spongy **soles**. The soles spread out as the camel walks to help support its weight in soft sand.

• On each foot, a camel has two toes. Its toe bones are broad, flat, and strong.

A Bactrian camel has a long neck with extralong fur that looks like a beard. Its eyes, ears, and nose are just right for its life in the desert. To keep out sand and dust, a camel has long, thick eyelashes and hair on the inside of its ears. In a storm, a camel closes its nostrils to keep out blowing sand. A camel has excellent senses of sight, hearing, and smell. It uses its super senses to check for danger in the distance.

LEATHERY LIPS

A camel has a large mouth and flexible, tough lips. With its leathery lips, it pulls thorny desert plants out of the stony soil without getting hurt. It uses its thirty-four strong, sharp teeth to grind up the rough food.

- A camel has large eyes and excellent vision.

- Its eyes are protected by a double row of long, curly eyelashes. They help keep out sand and dust and protect the camel's eyes from heat and cold.

- A camel's thick, bushy eyebrows shield its eyes from the desert Sun.

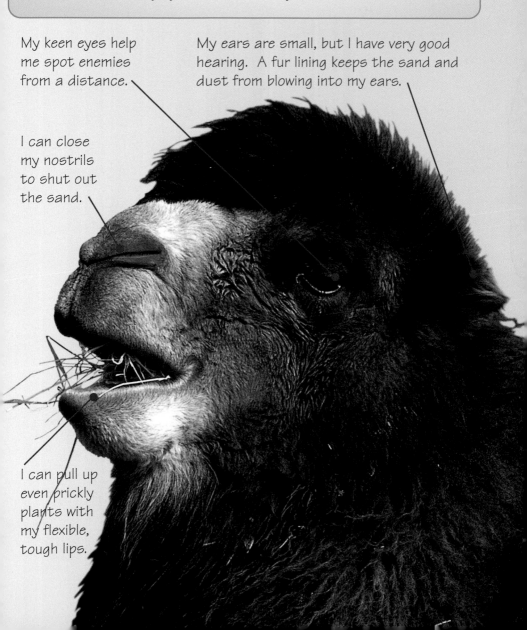

My keen eyes help me spot enemies from a distance.

My ears are small, but I have very good hearing. A fur lining keeps the sand and dust from blowing into my ears.

I can close my nostrils to shut out the sand.

I can pull up even prickly plants with my flexible, tough lips.

HOME, SWEET HOME

There are two different kinds of camels. One kind, the dromedary camel, has one hump. Dromedaries originally came from Arabia, but they were **domesticated** and now live in northern Africa, central Asia, and Australia. The other kind of camel, the Bactrian, has two humps. In the wild, Bactrians live only in the Gobi Desert in Asia. Herds of domestic Bactrians are kept by people who live in other parts of Asia, including Russia and China.

- Camels lived in North America about forty million to fifty million years ago. They **migrated** to Asia and Europe about two million years ago.

- Wild dromedary camels have become **extinct**, but some domestic dromedaries have returned to the wild in central Australia.

- Bactrian camels can survive in temperatures from an icy -17° Fahrenheit (-27° Celsius) to a scorching 122° F (50° C).

WHERE IN THE WORLD?

Bactrian camels live in the Gobi Desert. This huge desert stretches from the southern border of Russia, through Mongolia, and into parts of China. The Gobi is called a cold desert, but it really has extreme temperatures, from sweltering hot summers to freezing cold winters. Bactrian camels are well adapted to living in these harsh conditions.

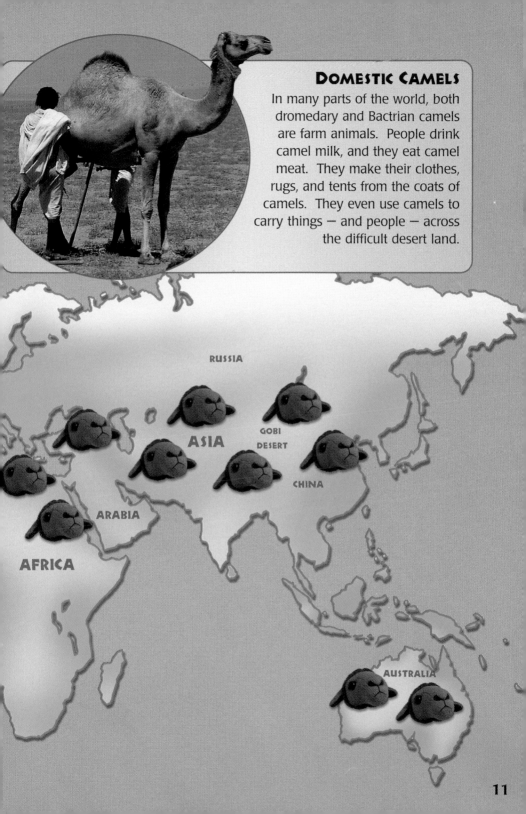

DOMESTIC CAMELS

In many parts of the world, both dromedary and Bactrian camels are farm animals. People drink camel milk, and they eat camel meat. They make their clothes, rugs, and tents from the coats of camels. They even use camels to carry things — and people — across the difficult desert land.

RUSSIA

ASIA

GOBI DESERT

CHINA

ARABIA

AFRICA

AUSTRALIA

Neighbors

A Bactrian camel's desert home is a bleak area with rocks, mountains, and drifting sand. This harsh **habitat** is home to many hardy animals. Gerbils and other small rodents rest in cool underground **burrows** during the hottest part of the day. After dark, they leave their burrows to search for food. Hawks, eagles, and other birds of prey fly above the desert at dawn and dusk looking for a meal. Small herds of wild horses and saiga antelope roam the plains, stopping to nibble the plants and grasses they find.

Hungry Hunters

Many birds of prey, such as this golden eagle, glide across the Gobi Desert. When they spot prey with their excellent eyesight, they swoop down and snatch it with their sharp talons.

NOSY ANTELOPE

A saiga antelope has a huge nose with a short, bendy trunk. The trunk is like a filter, stopping dust and sand from entering the antelope's lungs. In winter, a saiga's trunk warms the icy air so it can breathe more easily.

DID YOU KNOW?

Tiny Mongolian gerbils make homes in sandy burrows. At dusk, gerbils scurry around gathering seeds. It is not safe to stop and eat, so they stuff the seeds into their cheek pouches. When they have all they can carry, they take their meals to their burrows so they can eat slowly. Gerbils do not drink. They get all their water from their food.

THE FAMILY

Bactrian camels usually travel through the Gobi Desert in herds of about ten, led by the strongest male. Camels do not have a **territory**. Instead, camels move from place to place to find food and water, sometimes walking 30 miles (50 kilometers) in a single day. In summer, camels live in valleys and on nearby hills. In winter, they stay close to dry riverbeds, near **oases**.

Bactrian camels usually **mate** in February. Females give birth to the young, called calves, more than one year later. Newborn camels look like small adult camels. The females care for their calves for a few years. When young males reach about four years old, they leave their mothers to form herds with other young males. Females stay with their herds and raise calves of their own.

CHIEF CAMEL

Sometimes, a male dromedary camel (*top*) challenges the leader of a herd. The chief camel fights back, trying to bite or sit on his attacker. He may also show his anger by pushing out a red sac, shaped like a small balloon, from the corner of his mouth.

Baby File

Birth

A female camel usually gives birth to one calf at a time. At its birth, a camel calf weighs 70 to 88 pounds (32 to 40 kilograms). It has pale-colored, woolly fur, but it does not have humps yet. Unlike many types of animals, a camel calf is able to see at birth. Within one hour after its birth, it tries its first wobbly steps. After a few days of practice, it is able to keep up with the herd.

Six Months to One Year

The young camel grows quickly, feeding on its mother's rich milk. The calf begins to store fat, and its humps grow. Its coat slowly turns to a darker color. When a calf is about one year old, it no longer needs to drink milk from its mother, and it can find food on its own.

Two to Five Years

A calf stays near its mother until it becomes an adult at the age of three to five. Then male camels leave and form herds with other males. Young females begin to have their own calves, but they stay in their mothers' herds.

First Steps

A dromedary camel calf drinks the rich milk of its mother and grows quickly. Like a Bactrian calf, a dromedary calf is not born with a big hump. The hump gets larger as it fills with fat. A Bactrian has two humps, but a dromedary camel has just one hump.

LIFE IN THE DESERT

Living in the desert is tough. The temperature can be very hot or cold, and water can be hard to find. Camels, along with many other animals, have adapted to the harsh living conditions in the deserts of the world. Camels can survive for a long time without water. Other animals do not drink water at all because they get enough water from the food they eat. Camels can chew thorny desert plants that other animals are not tough enough to eat.

CLEVER COAT

The Bactrian camel's thick, shaggy coat keeps it warm in the winter snow. As the weather warms in spring, the Bactrian camel loses the fur from the underside of its body. It does not lose the thick fur on its back that protects the camel from the blazing summer Sun.

GOLDEN MOLE

Golden moles live under the warm desert sand in Africa. They have claws shaped like spades, or small shovels — just the right shape to burrow in sandy **dunes**. At night, golden moles search for their food. They cannot see, so they sniff around for the tasty lizards and insects they like to eat.

Frogs use their lungs and their skin to breathe. To breathe with their skin, they must keep it moist. Most frogs live in damp places, so keeping their skin moist is no problem. Finding a damp home is a problem, however, for a kind of frog that lives in burrows in the deserts of Australia. Known as the water-holding frog, it lives in its dry habitat by storing pockets of water under its skin.

SAND CAT

The sand cat lives in deserts in Africa and southwest Asia. To protect its feet from the heat and cold, it has thick fur on the underside of its paws. The fur also spreads the cat's weight so it can move more easily over the sand. This cat does not worry about looking for a drink. It gets the water it needs from its food, which it hunts at night.

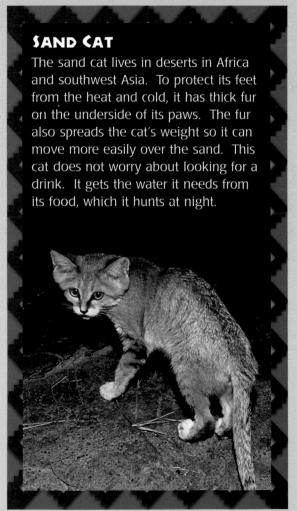

FAVORITE FOODS

Bactrian camels are **herbivores**. They eat any plants they find — even prickly plants. Hungry camels are not choosy. When plants are scarce, camels have been known to chew on bones, meat, and even sandals and tents! At an oasis, camels can eat their fill of lush green plants. After a feast, camels store extra food as fat in their humps. Then, when food is hard to find, camels live off the stored fat. A hump of a well-fed camel can weigh 80 pounds (36 kg).

CUD CHEWERS

Like domestic cows, a camel chews food twice. First, it swallows partly chewed plants. The food is kept in one part of its three-part stomach. Later, this food, called the **cud**, is brought back up, chewed carefully, and then swallowed again. Camels' teeth point forward so they quickly tear plants. Camels usually eat plants in the mornings and evenings and spend their afternoons chewing their cud.

Big Drinker

A camel can live without water more than five times as long as a person can. When a camel drinks, it can gulp more than 127 quarts (120 liters) of water in about ten minutes. If a camel cannot find freshwater, it can drink salty water.

Camels can be touchy! They sometimes spit the nasty-smelling contents of their stomachs at the things that annoy them. Frequent targets include **rival** camels and people.

Fatty Humps

A hungry camel is easy to spot. As a camel uses up the fat stored in its hump, the hump becomes thinner and flops over to one side.

DANGER!

Adult Bactrians have few enemies, although snow leopards and wolves do hunt camel calves. Humans are the main threat to wild camels. As people move into the once-wild areas of the Gobi Desert, they spoil the habitat for camels. Camels need lots of land where plants can grow. People build farms and villages on the land and let farm animals graze on the plants, leaving little food for wild camels.

SNOW LEOPARD

The rare and beautiful snow leopard is a fierce **predator**. It hunts mainly sheep, deer, and goats, but it kills young camels when it gets a chance. A snow leopard hunts by silently stalking its prey. When it gets close to its prey, it suddenly leaps. A snow leopard can leap as far as 50 feet (15 meters) in one bound. It also likes to sit on rocky ledges and attack its prey from above.

DID YOU KNOW?

Wild camels are in danger. There are lots of domestic Bactrian camels, but fewer than one thousand wild camels remain in the Gobi Desert. They are threatened with extinction.

WILY WOLF

Wolves hunt in packs of five to ten animals. They would not attack a healthy adult camel, but a calf makes a good meal for a family of hungry wolves.

SCARCE FOOD

At one time, Bactrian camels lived in many parts of Asia, but people with farm animals took over their land and food supply. Domestic dromedaries now eat the plants wild camels needed to survive.

A Camel's Day

5:00 AM The Sun had just risen. We needed to look for breakfast before it got too hot! My calf took a long drink of milk from her mother, and then we began to walk.

7:00 AM Food is scarce these days, but I found a patch of tough grass and small bushes for my herd to eat. As we ate our meal, my calf stayed close to her mother.

10:00 AM It was getting very hot as I led the herd toward the hills. We saw a herd of young males grazing. They grunted a greeting but did not bother us.

11:00 AM The calves in my herd were thirsty, so we stopped to let them drink some water. We nibbled on the few thorny bushes that grew among the rocks.

1:00 PM The herd rested. It was too hot to keep walking. There was no shade, but the thick fur on our backs protected us from the Sun.

2:00 PM We dozed and chewed our cud in the heat.

4:00 PM I saw the herd of males we had seen earlier. Two of them bit and spit at each other. Rivals can get into nasty fights.

24

5:00 PM We walked to a special spot in the foothills — a shady oasis. We all took a delicious drink of water, and we munched on grass and shrubs.

8:00 PM My calf took a long drink of milk and fell asleep. She and her mother huddled close to me. It was a lot cooler because the Sun had set.

10:00 PM My calf was asleep, and her mother was chewing her cud. I decided we would stay at the oasis for the night and rest. It was quiet, so I took a nap.

2:00 AM I woke up with a start. I listened carefully, but I couldn't hear anything. Sometimes wolves hunt here at night. We can't be too careful with little calves in the herd.

4:00 AM Another day will start soon. There is enough food here for breakfast, but then we will have to move on.

RELATIVES

The camel family is made up of two groups. Dromedary and Bactrian camels from Africa and Asia are one group. The other group includes guanacos, vicuñas, llamas, and alpacas, which all live in South America. The members of the camel family in South America are smaller than Asian and African camels, and they do not have humps. All of the members of the camel family have long, sturdy legs and feet made for walking on rocky ground or soft sand. They have slender necks, small heads, and **snouts**.

GUANACOS
Wild guanacos live in dry areas high in the Andes Mountains and on the lower plains. Guanacos, the largest mammals in South America, were once hunted for their thick, warm wool. In some areas now, there are laws against hunting guanacos.

CAMEL COUSINS

Like Bactrian camels, dromedary camels are well adapted for life in a desert habitat. For example, dromedaries in the Sahara Desert can live through a whole winter without water. Dromedaries are raised as domestic animals now, but they are no longer found in the wild.

HARDY AND FAST

A thick fur coat helps the vicuña live in its icy-cold home in the mountains of South America. A vicuña runs fast, reaching speeds of up to 28 miles (45 km) per hour as it races across its rocky home.

DID YOU KNOW?

Camel spiders are not related to camels, but just like camels, they live in dry places. Camel spiders are not spiders either, but they are close relatives. Camel spiders grow to about 4 inches (10 centimeters) wide. They have eight legs and run fast. Camel spiders are fierce nighttime predators that hunt scorpions, mice, and reptiles such as lizards.

HUMANS AND CAMELS

Many people who live in deserts depend on camels for transportation and food. For thousands of years, people have used camels to carry things and to work on farms. Camels also provide their owners with food, shelter, and clothing. People make leather goods from camel hides and fabric for clothes and tents from camel fur. In some places, the number of camels a family owns shows how wealthy the family is.

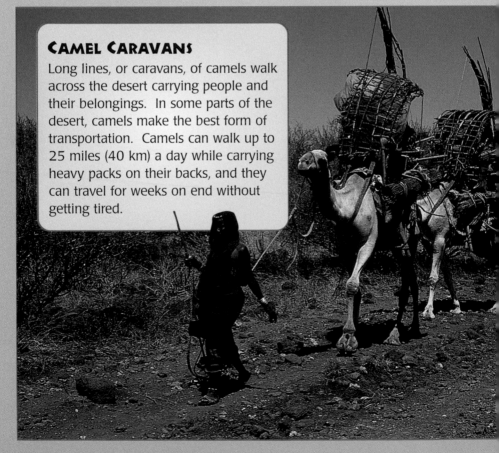

CAMEL CARAVANS

Long lines, or caravans, of camels walk across the desert carrying people and their belongings. In some parts of the desert, camels make the best form of transportation. Camels can walk up to 25 miles (40 km) a day while carrying heavy packs on their backs, and they can travel for weeks on end without getting tired.

Rapid Racers

Camel racing is a popular sport in many areas, such as the Middle East and Australia. The camels are specially raised just for racing and are ridden by trained jockeys. They can run as fast as racehorses.

DID YOU KNOW?

- Camels can pull heavy loads, but they are unpredictable and may kick and spit at people who pile on too much.

- In some areas, camel **dung** is used as fuel for fires.

- Cloth made of camel fur is sold in many parts of the world. It is used to make blankets, coats, and suits.

Camel Milk

Cows do not live deep in Asian or African deserts. In the desert, people milk camels instead. Camel milk is a very healthy food, containing more nutrients than milk from cows. Camel milk can also be made into cheese.

Glossary

ADAPTED
Adjusted to certain conditions.

BURROWS
Tunnels or holes in the ground used as shelter by animals.

CUD
The partly digested food that is brought up from the stomach to be chewed again by camels and some other animals.

DOMESTICATED
Trained or tamed to live with humans.

DUNES
Large drifts of sand shaped by the wind.

DUNG
The solid waste produced by an animal; manure.

EXTINCT
No longer in existence.

HABITAT
The natural setting in which plants and animals live.

HERBIVORES
Animals that eat only plants.

MATE
To come together for the purpose of producing young.

MIGRATED
Moved from one country or area to another.

OASES
Places in a desert where water is found and plants often grow.

PREDATOR
An animal that hunts other animals for food.

RIVAL
Having the same goals as another individual or being in competition with another.

SCARCE
Rare and hard to find.

SNOUTS
Long noses that stick out from animals' heads.

SOLES
The bottom part of feet.

TERRITORY
A large area of land claimed by someone or something for a particular use.

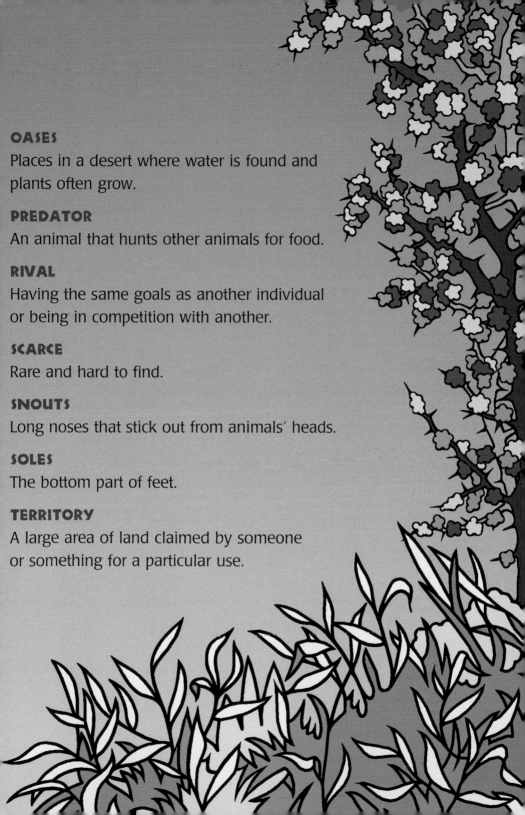

INDEX